ANIMAL DETECTIVES / DETECTIVES DEL REINO ANIMAL

MILITARY DOLPHINS
DELFINES DEL EJÉRCITO

Rosie Albright

Traducción al español: Eduardo Alamán

PowerKiDS
press™

New York

Published in 2012 by The Rosen Publishing Group, Inc.
29 East 21st Street, New York, NY 10010

First Edition

Editor: Joanne Randolph   Traducción al español: Eduardo Alamán
Designer: Kate Laczynski

Photo Credits: Cover, pp. 10, 12–13, 17, 24 (bite plate, handler) © Louise Murray/age fotostock; pp. 5, 14, 18 Shutterstock.com; p. 6 © www.iStockphoto.com/Alexey Tkachenko; p. 9 Brien Aho/U.S. Navy/Getty Images; pp. 21, 24 (waterway) Frank Rossoto Stocktrek/Getty Images; p. 22 U.S. Navy/Getty Images.

Library of Congress Cataloging-in-Publication Data

Albright, Rosie.
 Military dolphins = Delfines del ejército / by Rosie Albright. — 1st ed.
    p. cm. — (Animal detectives, Detectives del reino animal)
 Parallel title: Delfines del ejército
 Includes index.
 Text in English and Spanish.
 ISBN 978-1-4488-6716-5 (library binding)
 1. Bottlenose dolphin—War use—Juvenile literature. 2. United States. Navy—Juvenile literature. I. Title. II. Title: Delfines del ejército. III. Series.
 UH100.5.B68A4318 2012
 359.4'24—dc23
                                    2011025894

Web Sites: Due to the changing nature of Internet links, PowerKids Press has developed an online list of Web sites related to the subject of this book. This site is updated regularly. Please use this link to access the list:
www.powerkidslinks.com/andt/dolphin/

Manufactured in the United States of America

CPSIA Compliance Information: Batch #WW12PK: For Further Information contact Rosen Publishing, New York, New York at 1-800-237-9932

CONTENTS

CONTENIDO

Dolphins are smart. They
are easy to train, too.

Los delfines son inteligentes.
Los delfines son fáciles
de entrenar.

Dolphins are trained using food. When they learn new skills, they get fish.

A los delfines se les entrena usando comida. Cuando aprenden un truco les dan pescado.

The Navy and Marines train dolphins. The trained dolphins are called military dolphins.

La marina y el ejército entrenan delfines. A estos delfines se les llama delfines militares.

The person who trains a military dolphin is its **handler**.

A la persona que entrena los delfines militares se le conoce como **entrenador**.

Military dolphins are trained in San Diego, California. The dolphins live in special pens.

Estos delfines se entrenan en San Diego, California. Los delfines viven en corrales especiales.

Military dolphins look for mines in the water. They use special tools to mark the mines.

Los delfines militares buscan minas en el agua. Los delfines usan herramientas especiales para marcar las minas.

Dolphins hold most tools with their mouths. The part they hold is called the **bite plate**.

Los delfines sujetan las herramientas con la boca. La parte que sujetan se llama **placa de mordida.**

17

Military dolphins look for enemy swimmers, too. Then naval officers can stop them from hurting people.

Los delfines militares también buscan enemigos en el agua. Así los oficiales navales pueden evitar que hagan daño.

Dolphins keep **waterways** safe during wars. Supplies can get to people who need them.

Los delfines mantienen seguras las **vías maritimas** durante las guerras. Así las provisiones pueden llegar a las personas que las necesitan.

Military dolphins have been used in the war in Iraq. They have saved many lives.

Los delfines militares se han usado en la guerra de Irak. Los delfines han salvado muchas vidas.

Words to Know / Palabras que debes saber

**bite plate /
(la) placa
de mordida**

**handler /
(el/la)
entrenador(a)**

**waterway /
(las) vías
marítimas**

Index

Índice